RED LEGS

A DRUMMER BOY OF THE CIVIL WAR

Written and illustrated by Ted Lewin

HarperCollins*Publishers*

Red Legs: A Drummer Boy of the Civil War. Copyright © 2001 by Ted Lewin. Printed in the U.S.A. All rights reserved. www.harperchildrens.com
Library of Congress Cataloging-in-Publication Data. Lewin, Ted.   Red Legs : a drummer boy of the Civil War / by Ted Lewin.
p.   cm.   Summary: A young boy participates in a Civil War reenactment with his father.   ISBN 0-688-16024-7 — ISBN 0-688-16025-5 (lib. bdg.)
1. Child soldiers—United States—History—19th Century—Juvenile literature. 2. Historical reenactments—United States—Juvenile literature.
3. United States—History—Civil War, 1861–1865—Participation, Juvenile—Juvenile literature. I. Title. E540.C47 L49 2001 00-32046
[E]—dc21 Typography by Robbin Gourley 1 2 3 4 5 6 7 8 9 10 ❖   First Edition   This type is set at 18/26 pt. Caslon Bold.

★ ★ ★ ★ ★ ★ ★ ★ ★ ★ ★ ★ ★ ★ ★ ★ ★

For drummer boy Justin Caliguri
and his father, Mike. Special thanks to the men
of Companies E, C, and H, 14th Brooklyn.

★ ★ ★ ★ ★ ★ ★ ★ ★ ★ ★ ★ ★ ★ ★ ★ ★

Stephen sits gazing into the flames.
He is a long way from home.
He composes a letter in his mind:

Dear Mother,
    We have come very far and are bone-tired, but the Red Legs are in good spirits. We are encamped in a wood just above the battlefield. I sleep on a bed of straw. We sing songs each night around the fire. It makes us feel good.

Tomorrow our two great armies will face each other. Some of the men have brothers on the other side. We have drilled hard and are ready. I hope I am brave. I may be only nine, but I want to do my part to save the Union. I will try to make you proud.

Your loving son,
Stephen

The next morning, Stephen and the men, weary from their long march, rouse themselves from sleep and put on their jackets and kepis (caps). It is time to line up for roll call.

After a breakfast of slab bacon and coffee,
they sit and talk of home. Shafts of sunlight
slant through the trees. A woodpecker drums
and blue jays screech.

A bugle blares the officers' call. The sergeant orders Stephen to sound assembly. Stephen's heart pounds as he collects the drumsticks from his tent. He adjusts his drum and beats:

Ratta-TAT, ratta-TAT, ratta-TAT-TAT-TAT. Ratta-TAT, ratta-TAT, ratta-TAT-TAT-TAT.

The Red Legs muster, along with the other units.

Stephen and the other drummer boys beat a steady tattoo on their drums. Thousands of feet thump to the rhythm. The soldiers are marching to battle.

In the Confederate camp, thousands of men and boys dressed in butternut homespuns march to the beat of their drums and the spine-tingling whistle of fifes playing "Dixie."

Puffs of smoke rise from the tree line. The thunder of cannon
fire shakes the earth. Flags flutter and snap in the smoke and dust.

The drummer boys are sent to the rear. From the hill where they stand, they watch wave after wave of men led by officers on horseback charge and fall in the withering fire.

Still they come, running now, muskets piercing the sky.

The fighting roar of men's voices wells up above the boom of cannon.

The cavalry units charge at full gallop.

The troopers wield long sabers.

The Confederate lines send off a terrible volley. Stephen falls. A red spot wells up on the white strap of his drum, just over his heart.

"Cease fire!" a voice calls out. The shooting stops.

The mournful wail of taps drifts over the smoke of the battle.

A hand reaches down.

Stephen's father helps him up. He and the others around him rise.
They brush the dust and grass off their uniforms.

They shake hands with the enemy. The battle is over. They can all
go home because . . .

. . . this battle was a reenactment of a Civil War battle. When it is over, Stephen gets up and goes home. During the Civil War, 100,000 child soldiers did not get up and go home. They never went home. They were among the 700,000 who perished in the four years of that bloody conflict.

Stephen and his father are reenactors, or living historians as they call themselves. They dress in authentic uniforms, use real weapons, and even put on make-believe blood to re-create the battles where they happened, as they happened. Reenactors do it because they love history and wish to honor the memory of the men and boys on both sides who died fighting so long ago.

The story of this drummer boy is based on the life of Stephen Benjamin Bartow (b. 1846), a musician in the 14th Regiment, Company E, a unit from Brooklyn, New York. Stephen and the soldiers of the 14th Brooklyn, as they were more commonly known, were called the Red-Legged Devils by the Confederate general Stonewall Jackson because of the color of their uniform and their tough fighting spirit. Stephen fought in twenty-two battles, including the battles at Gettysburg and Bull Run.

Stephen enlisted in September 1862 and served three years. In this story, Stephen "dies." In real life, however, Stephen survived the war, became a mason, and helped build the Brooklyn Bridge. In 1911, he died in Brooklyn at the age of sixty-five, just blocks away from where the author now lives.